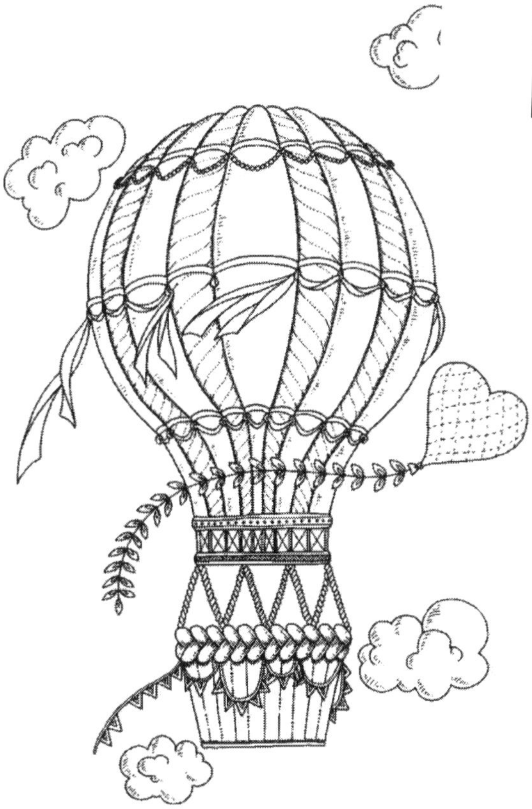

BALLOON PUBLISHING

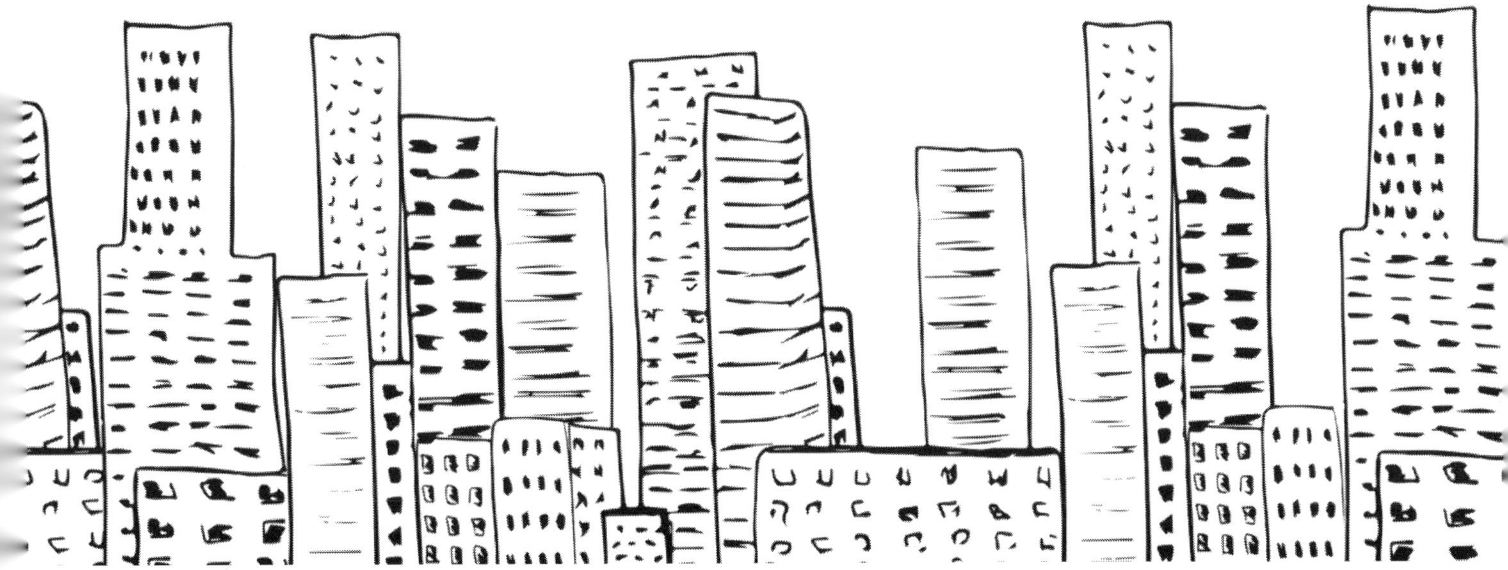

COLOR TEST PAGE

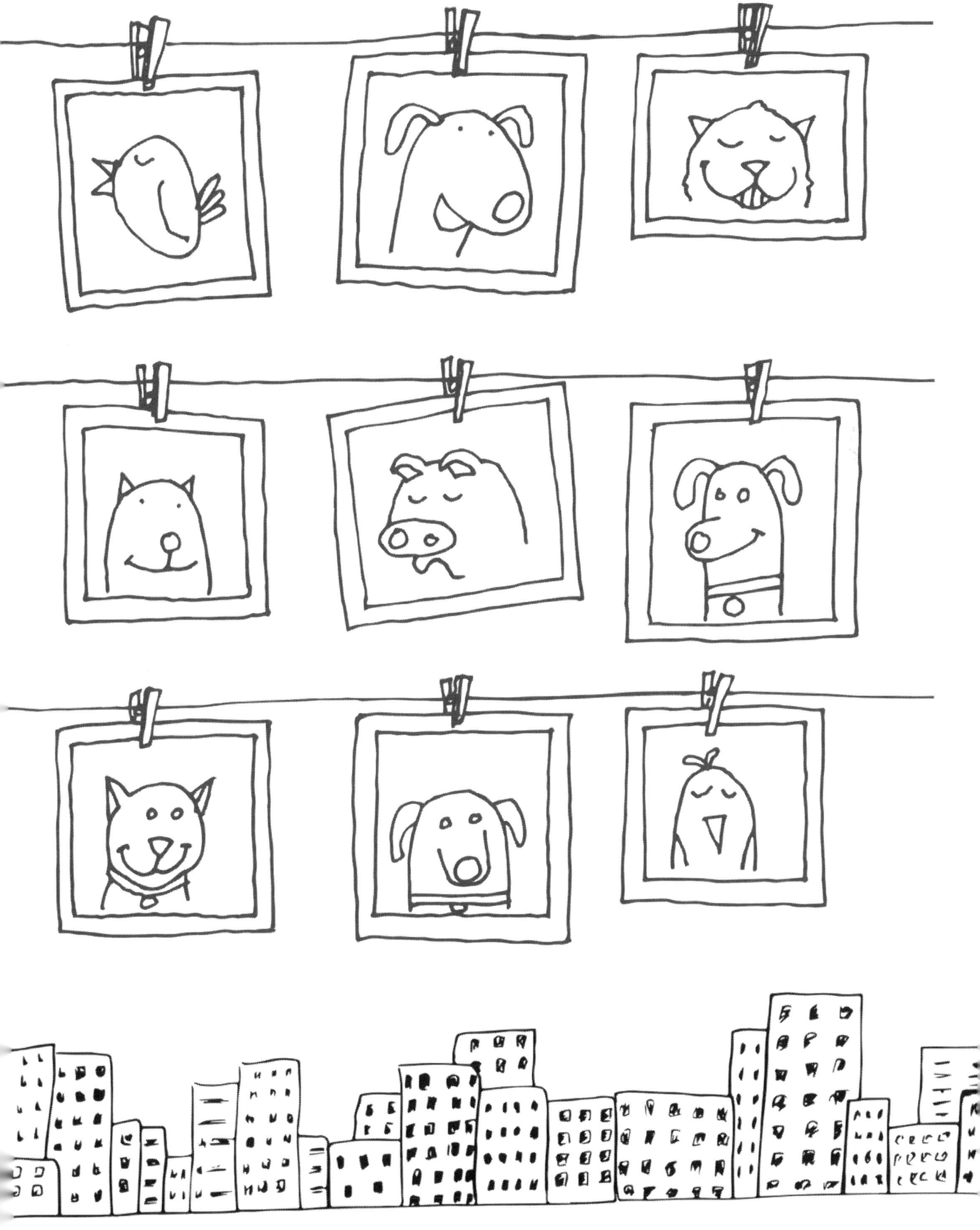

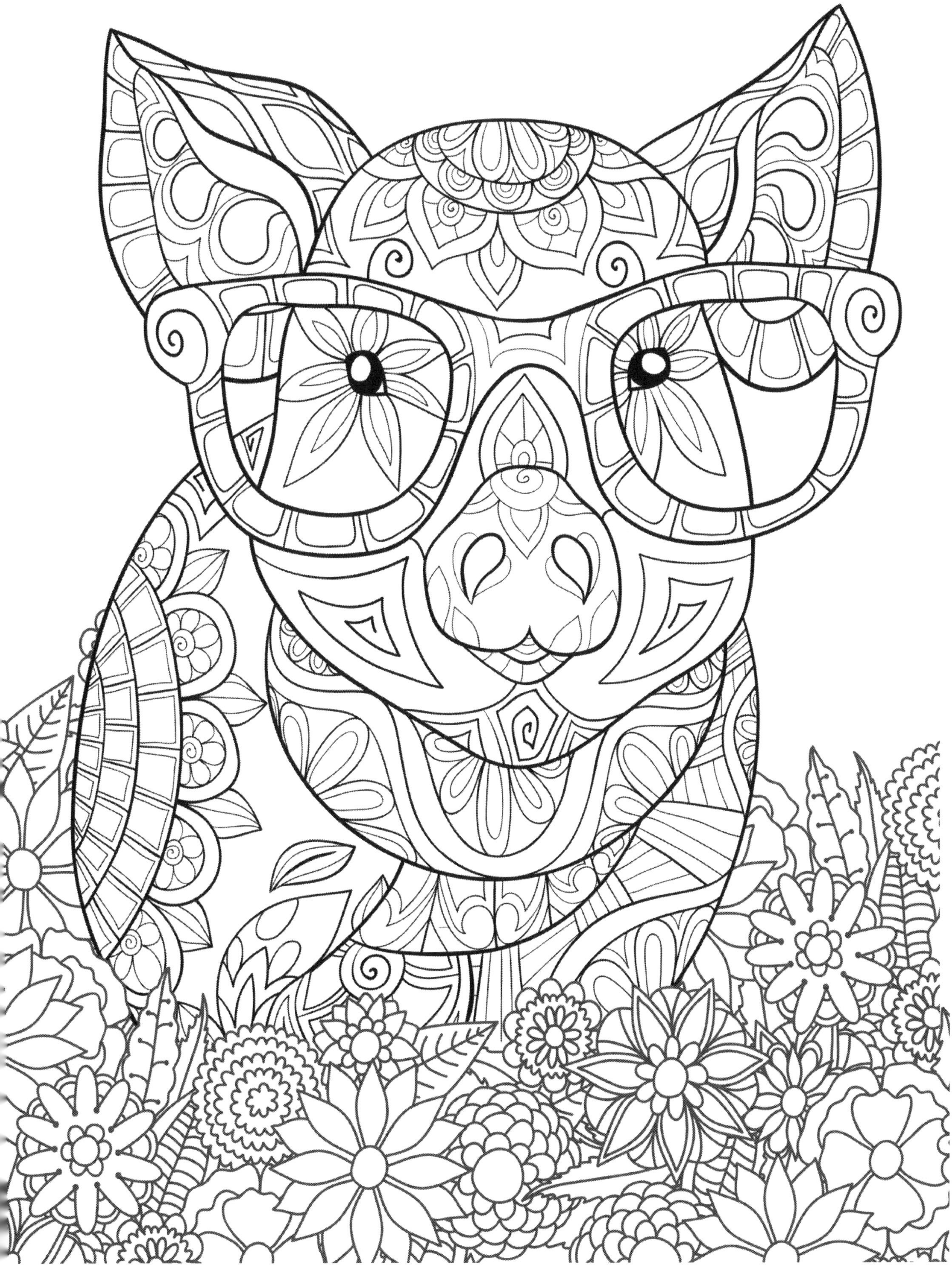

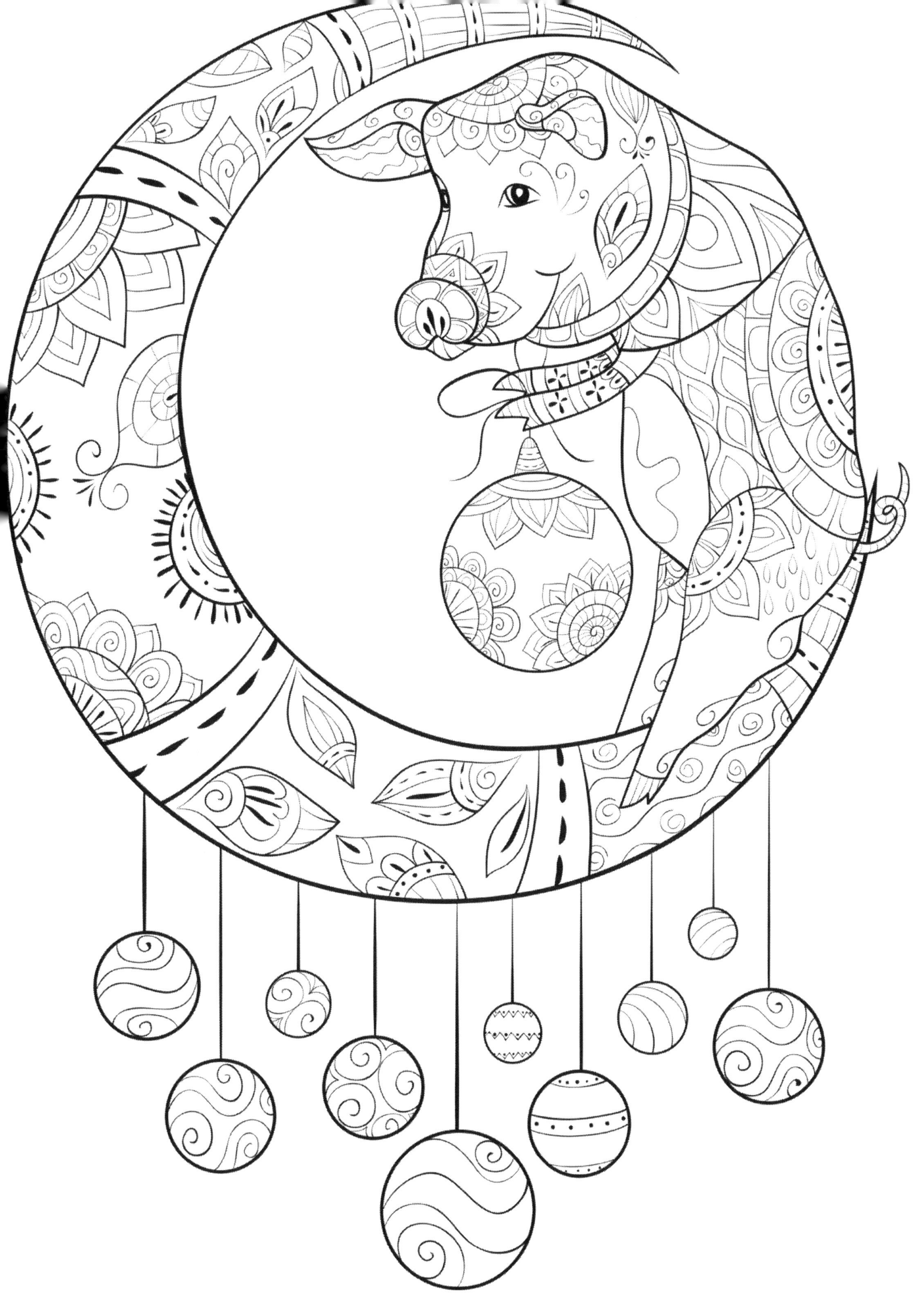

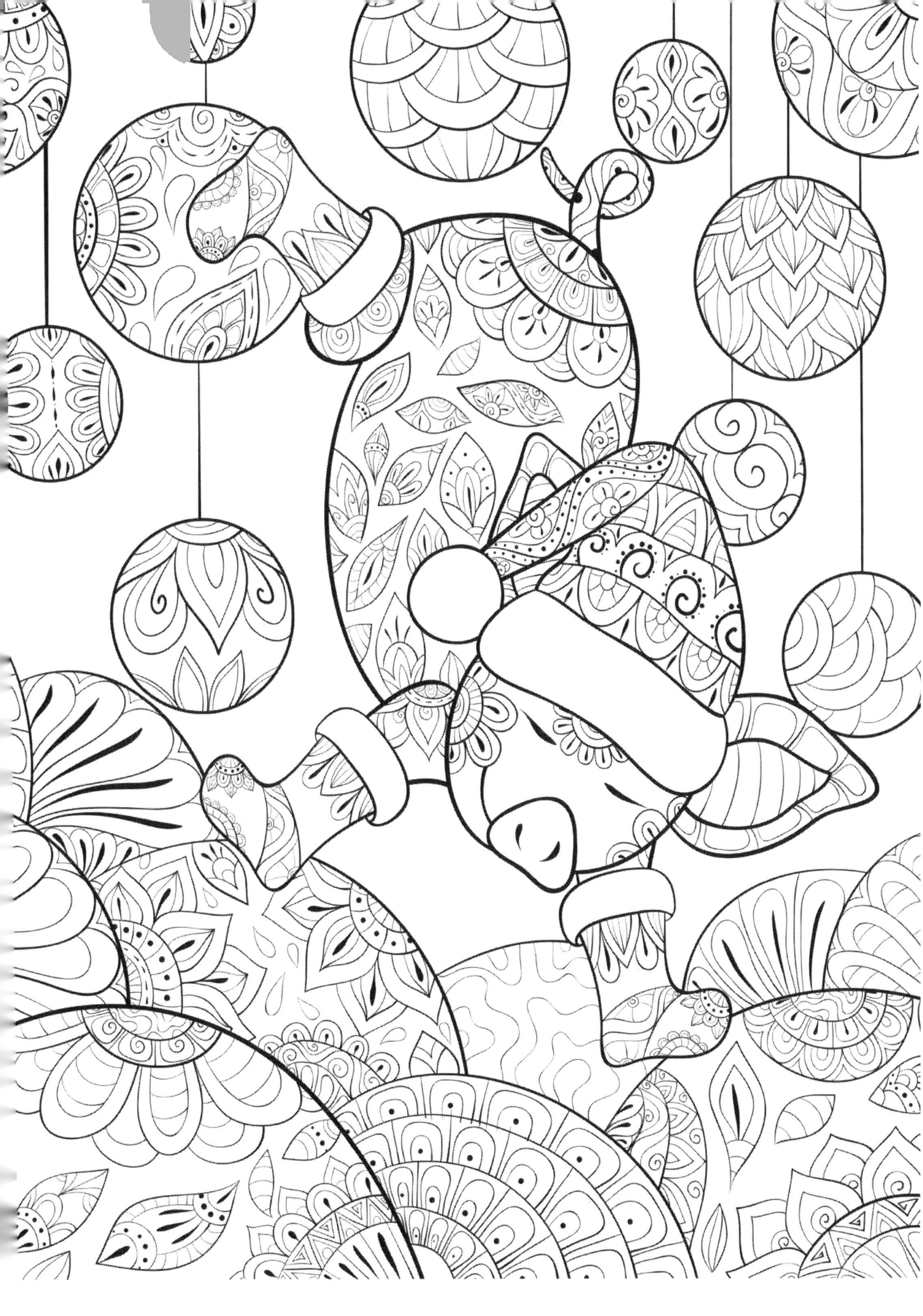

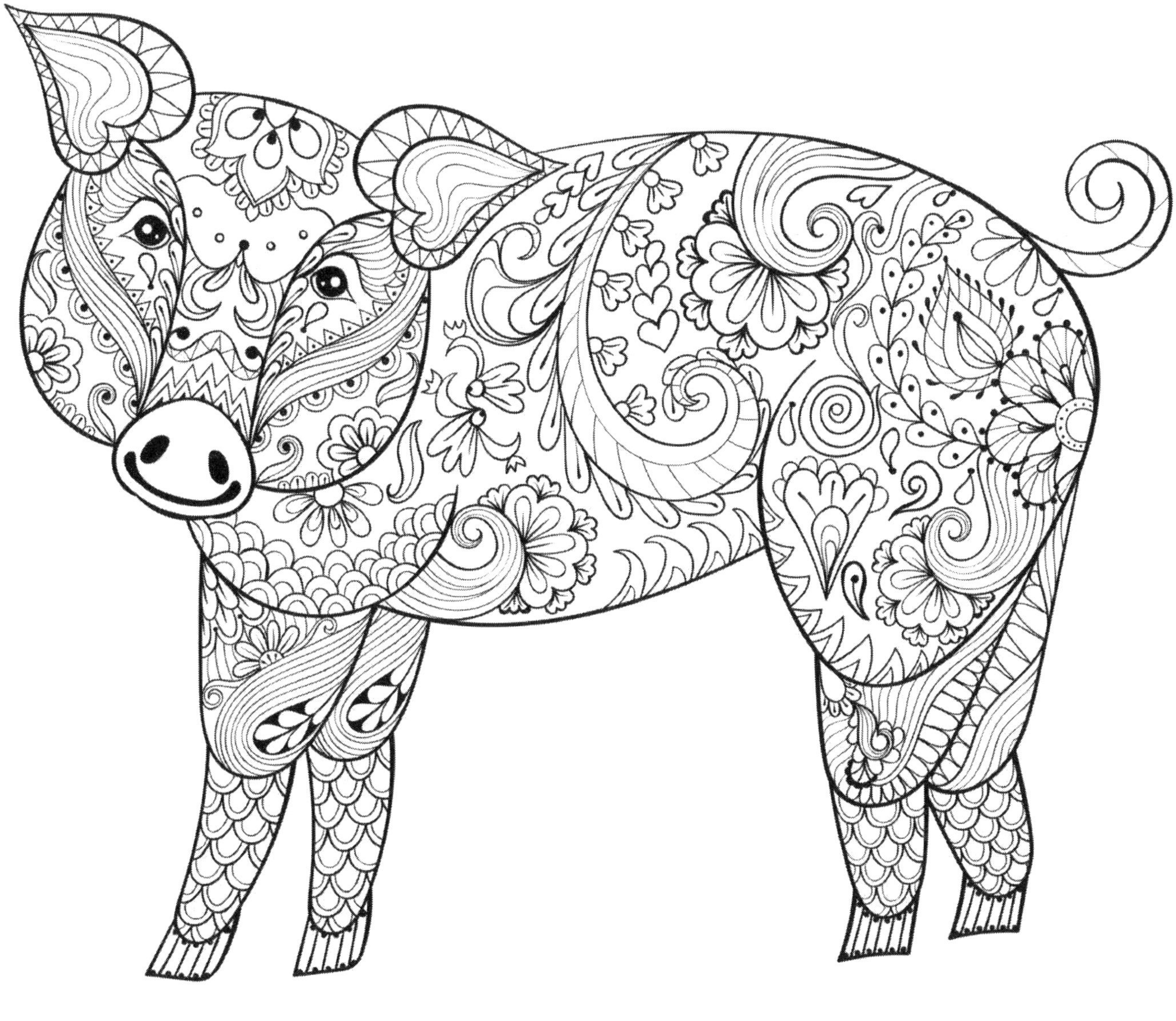

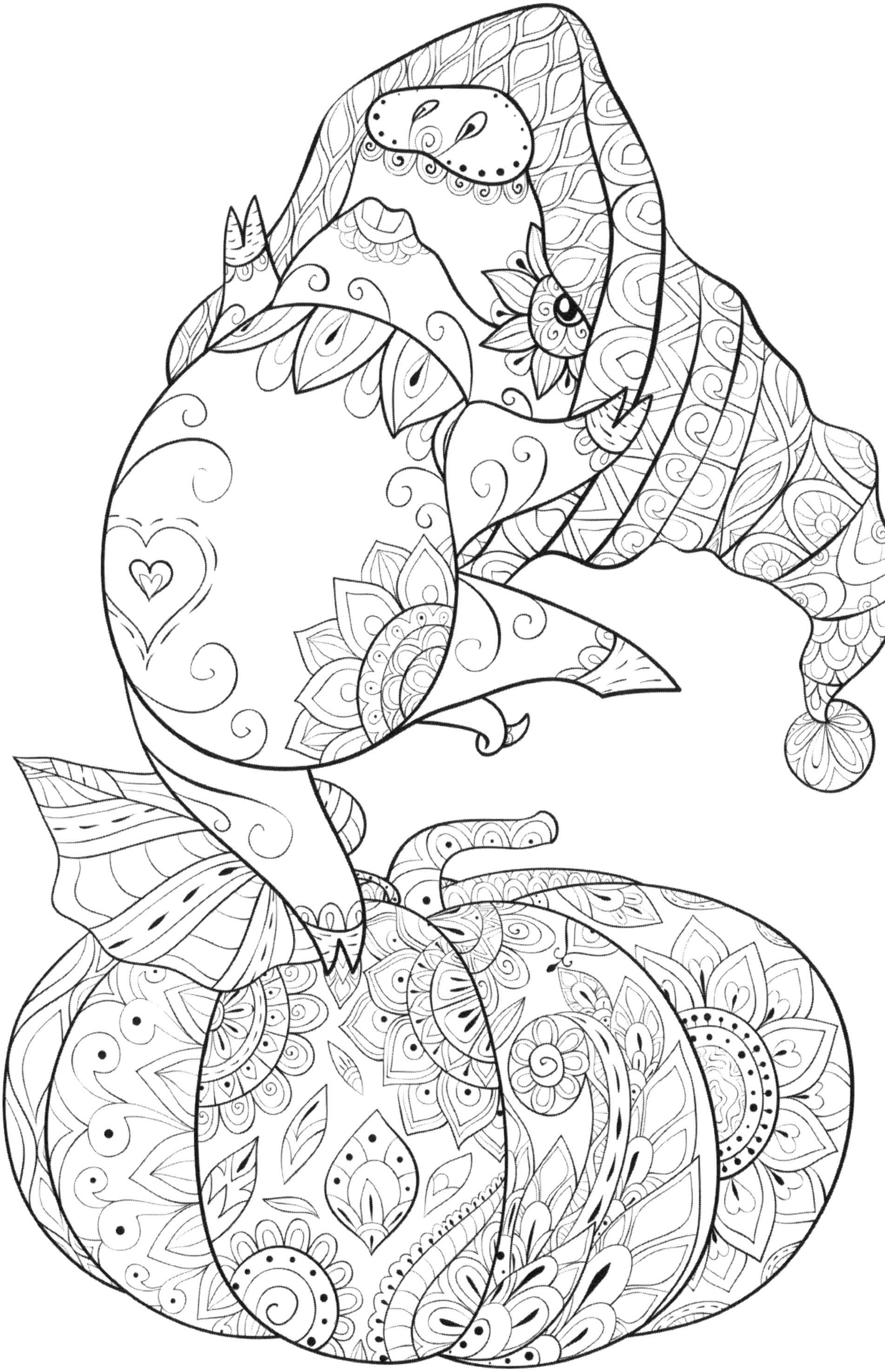

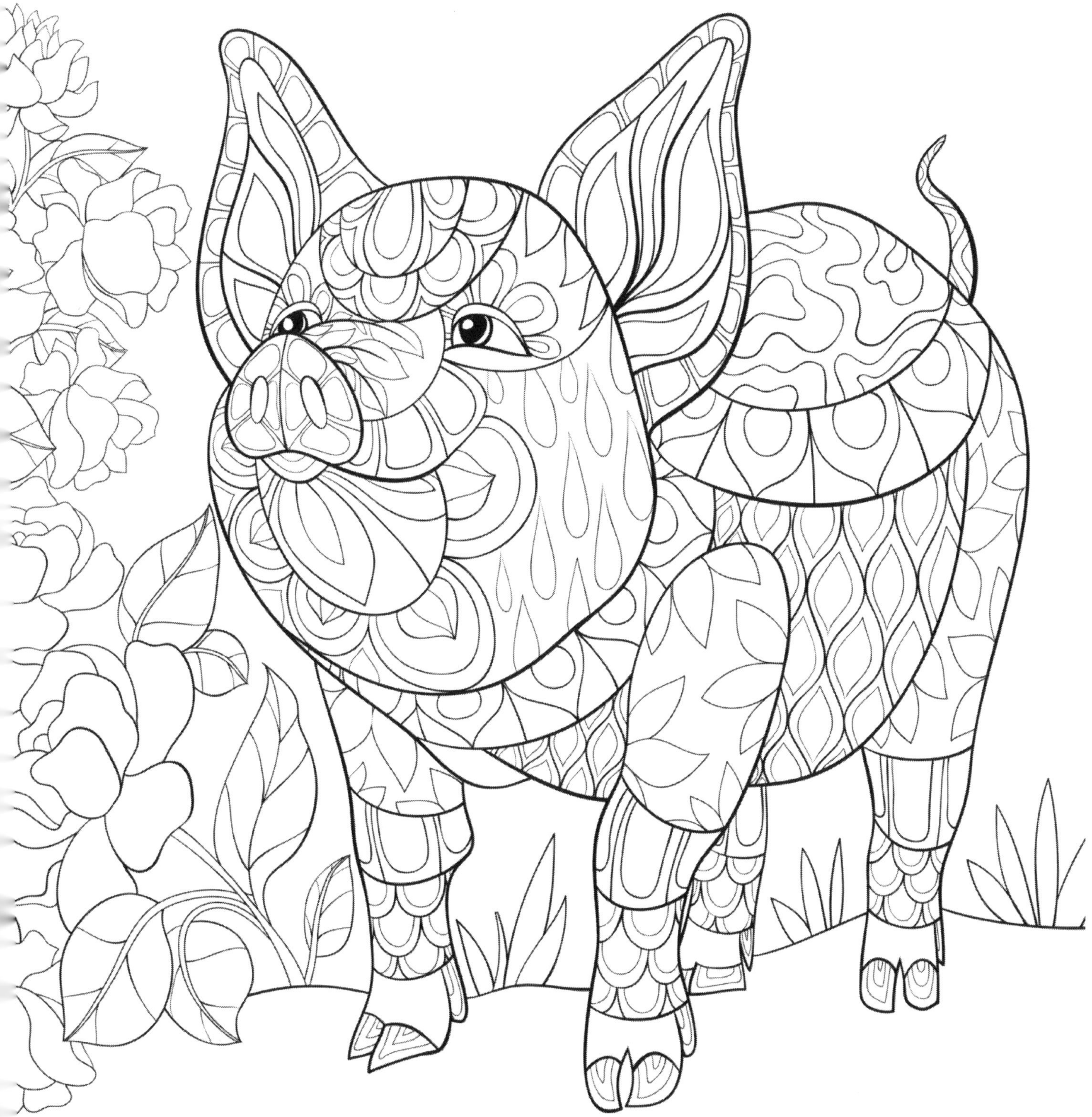

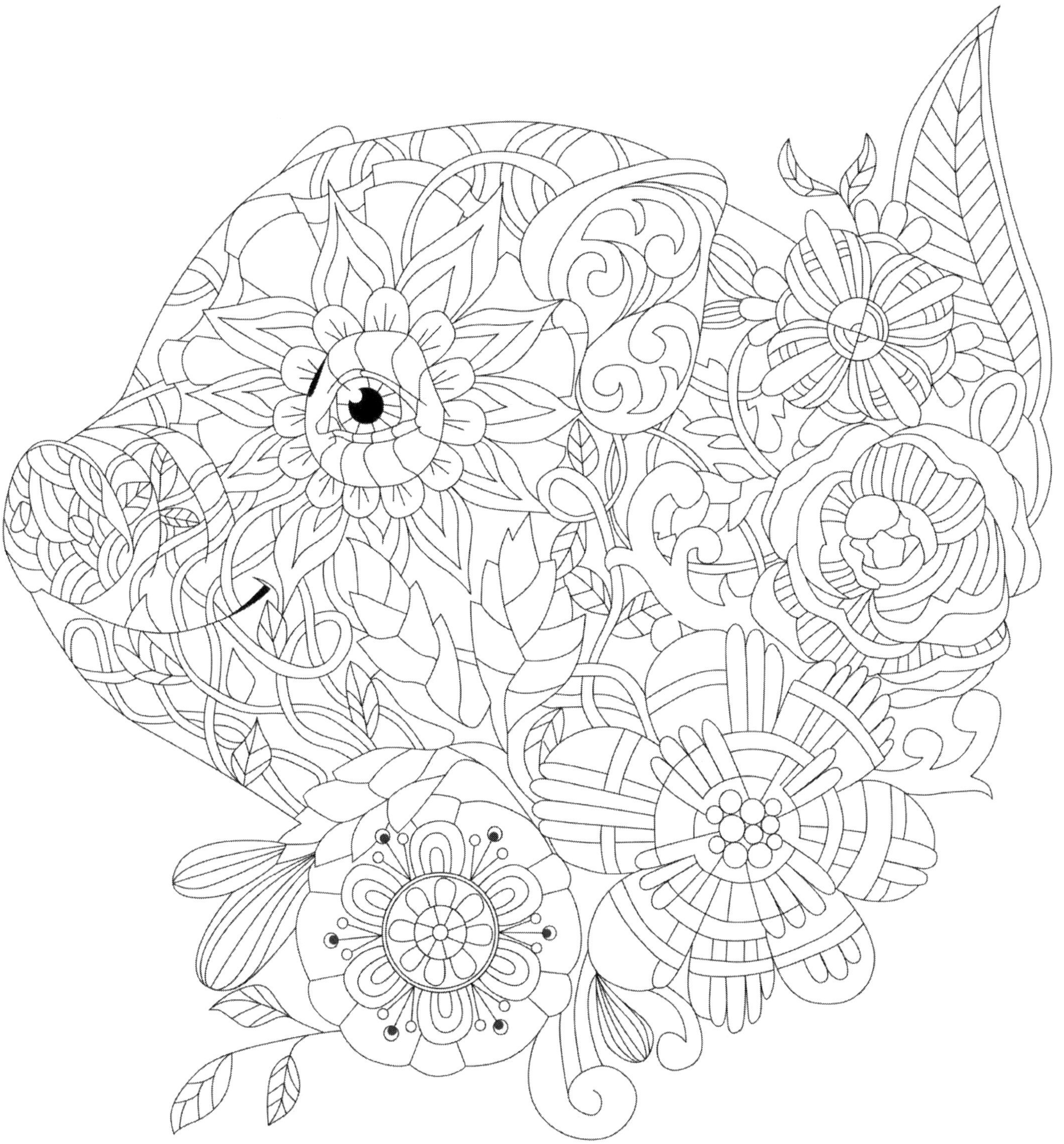

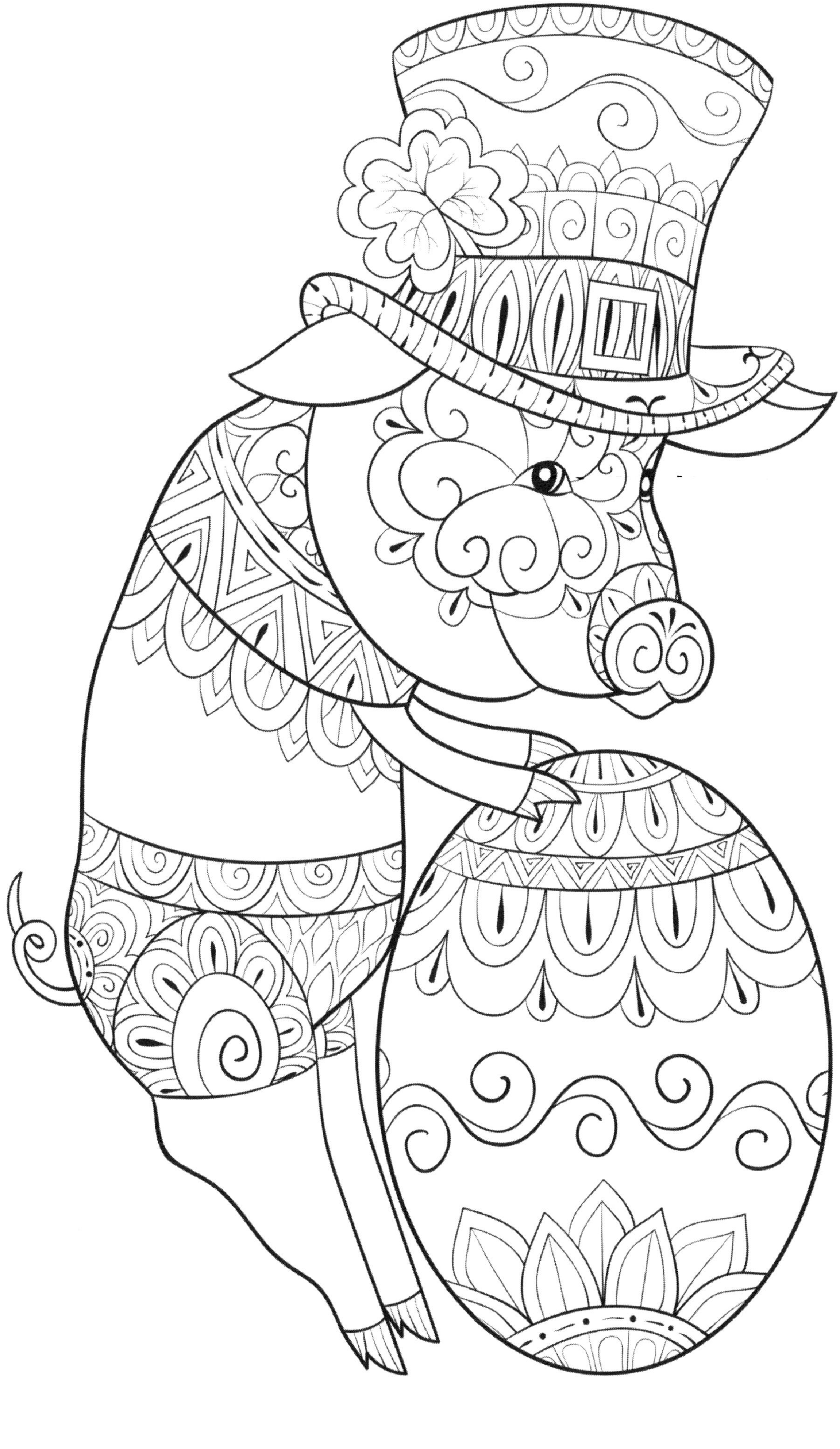

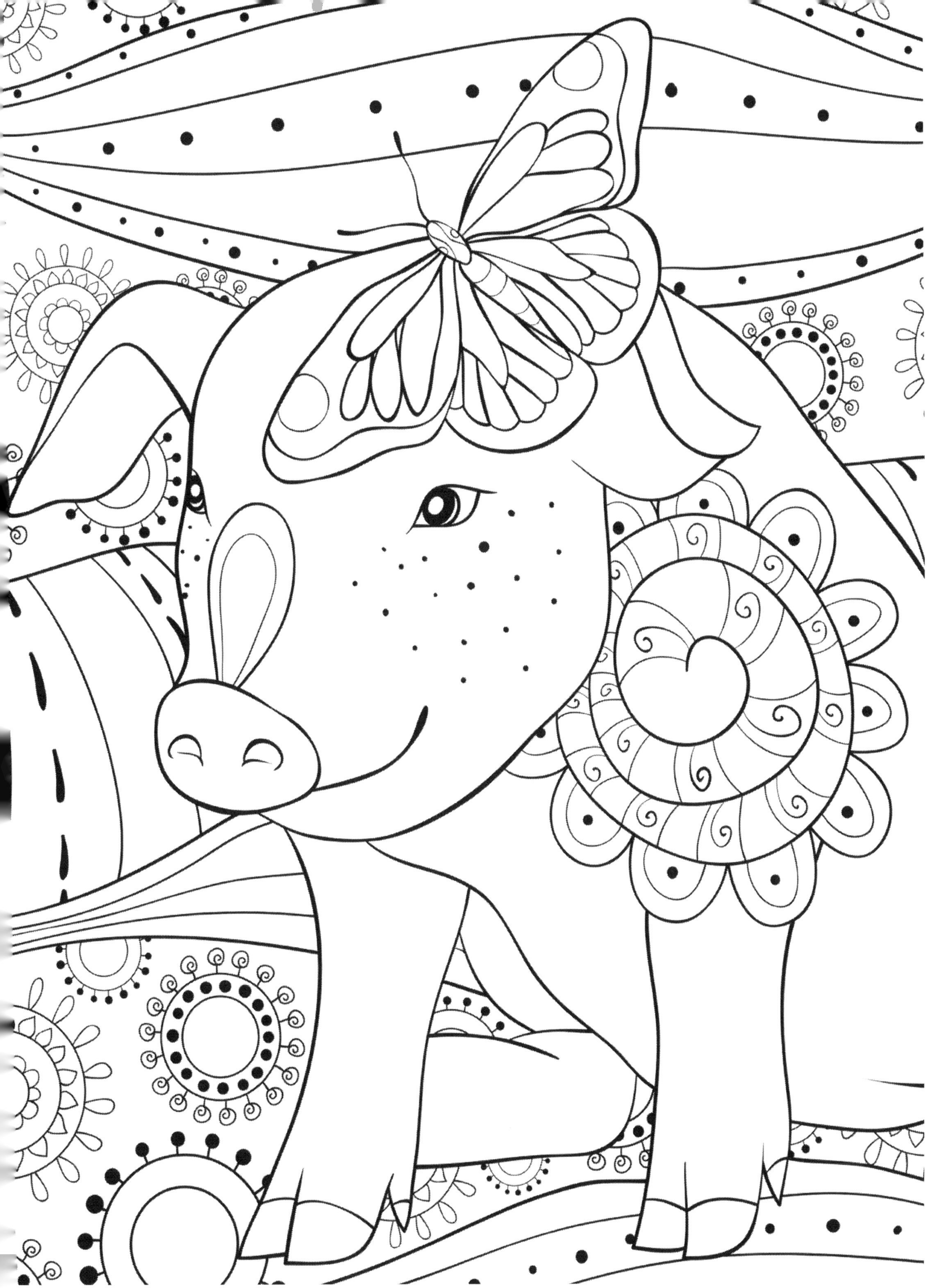

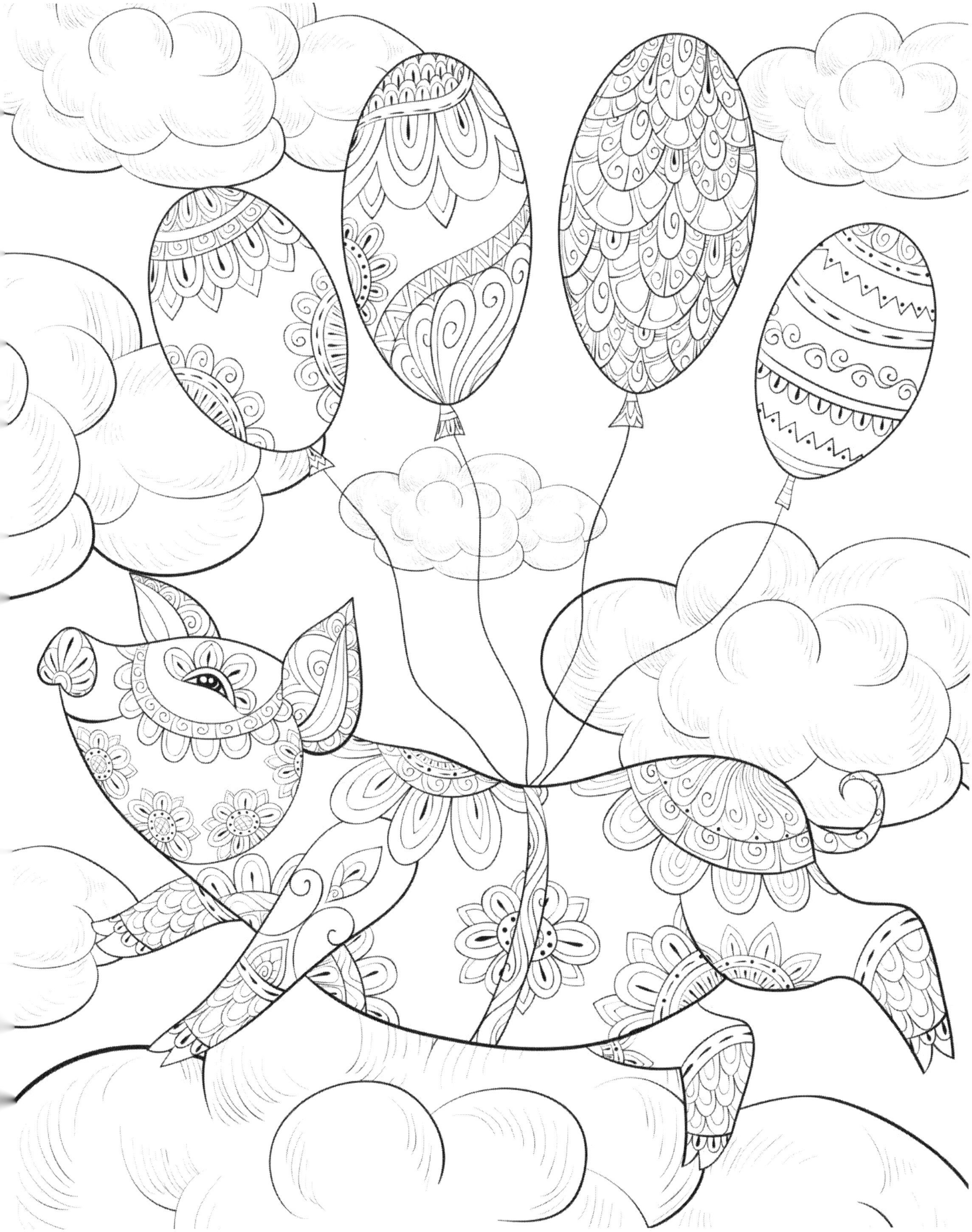

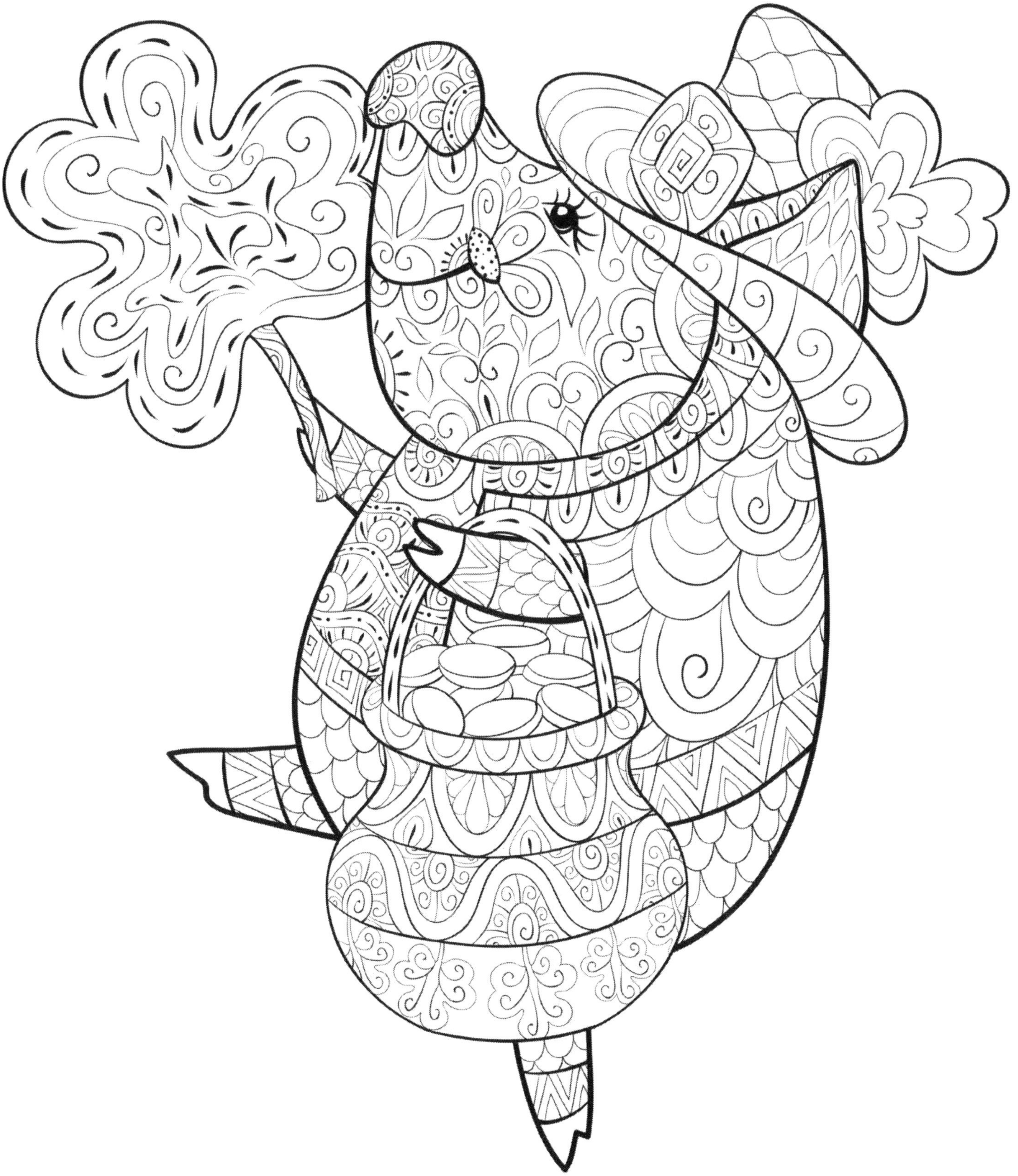

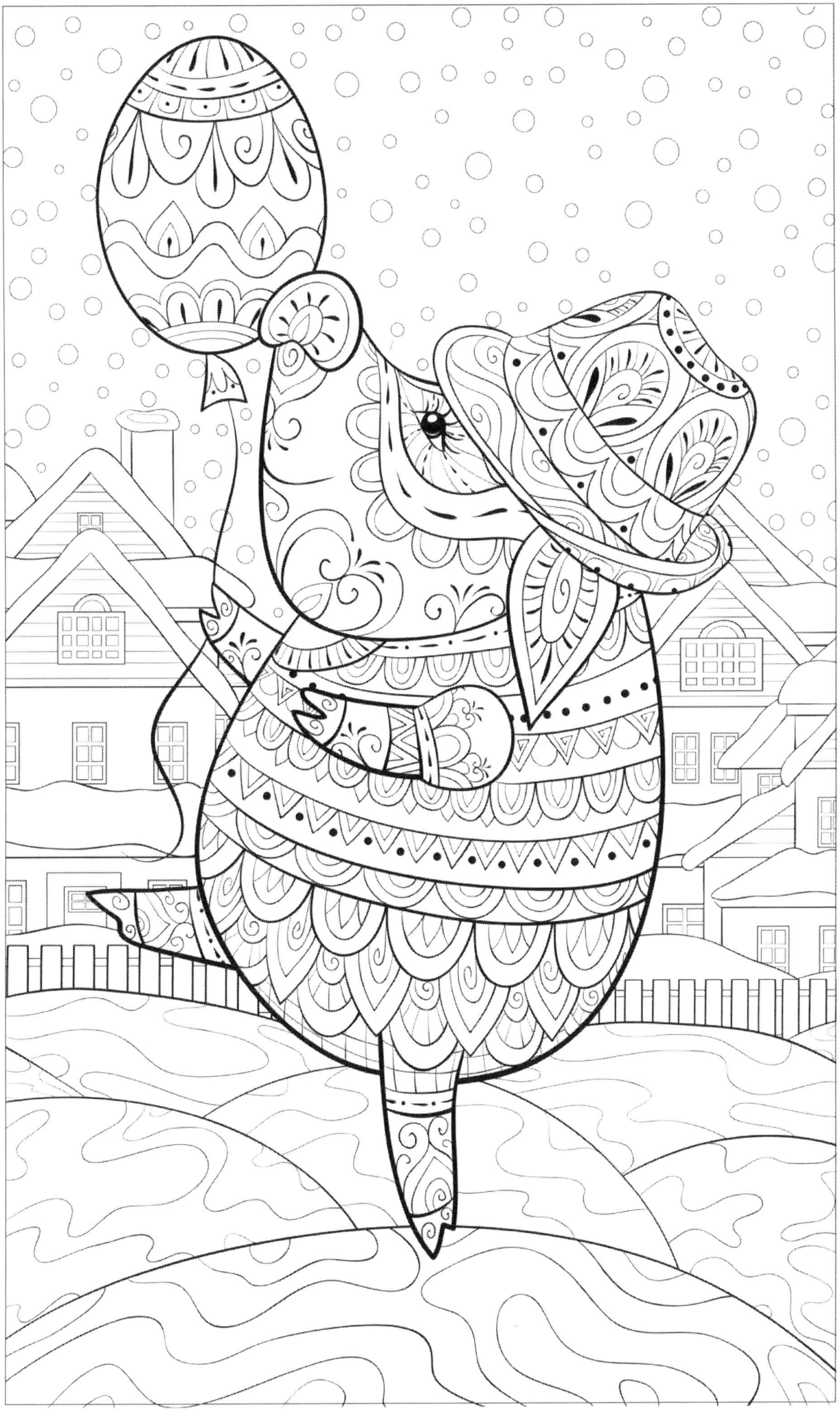

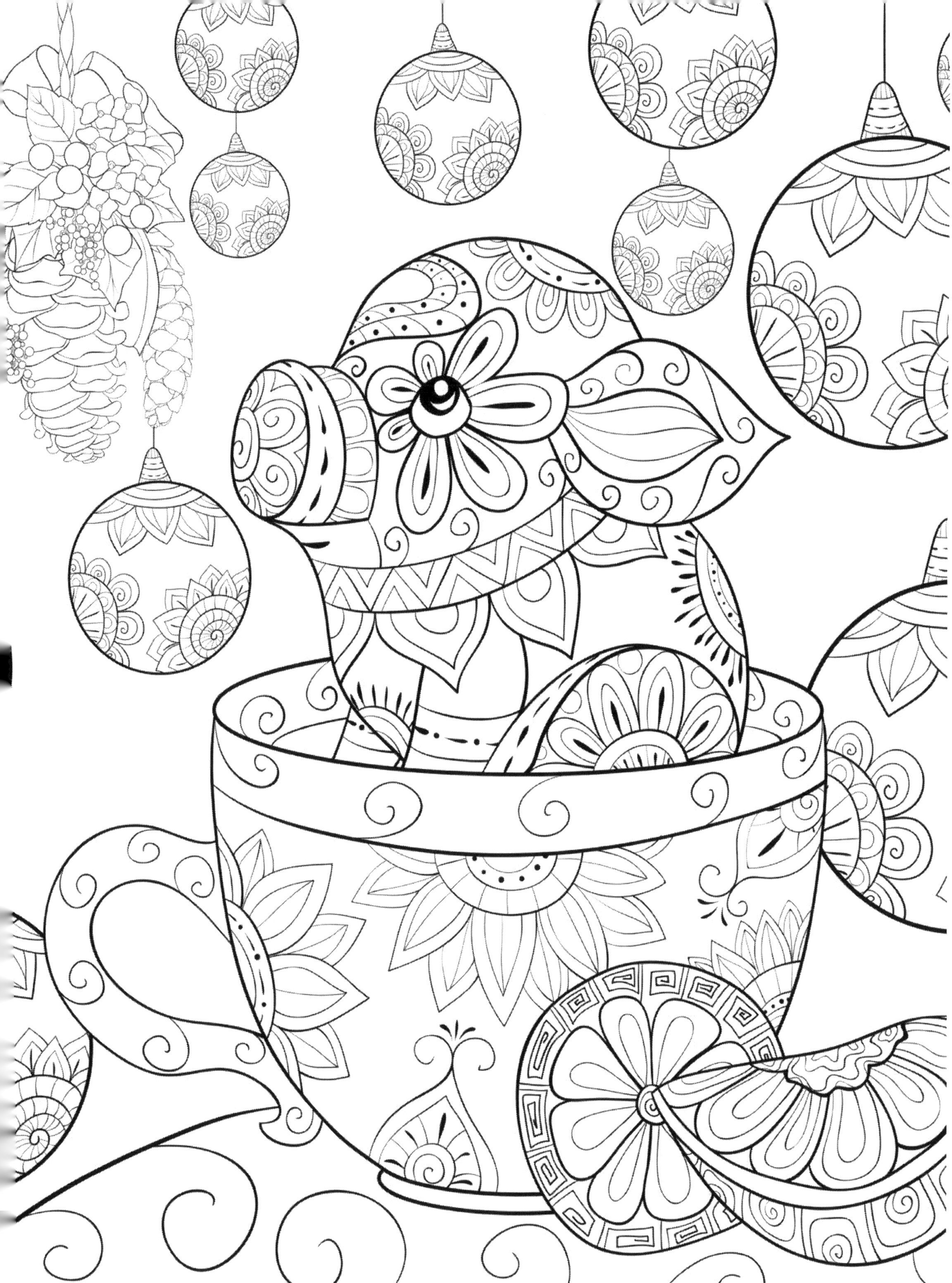

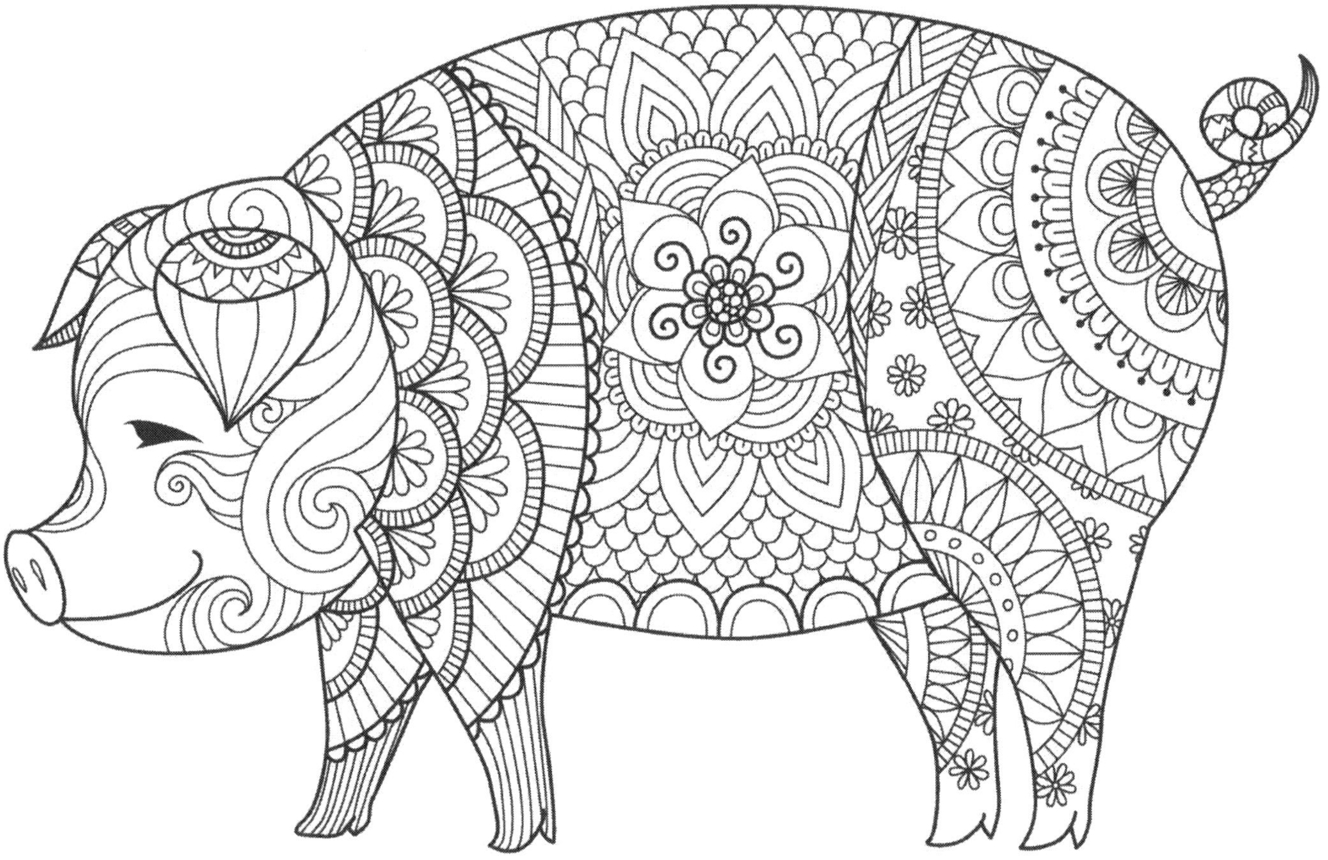

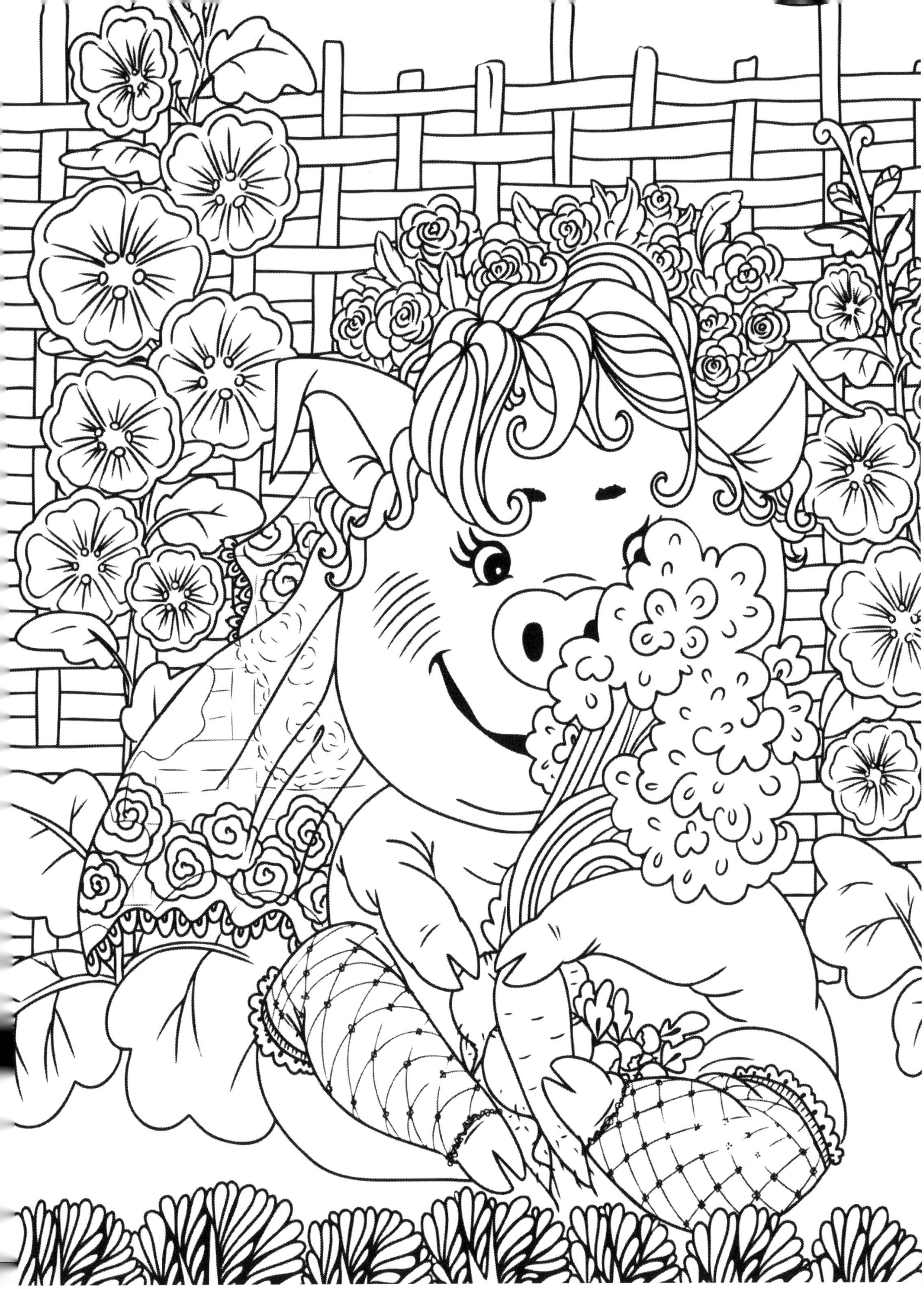

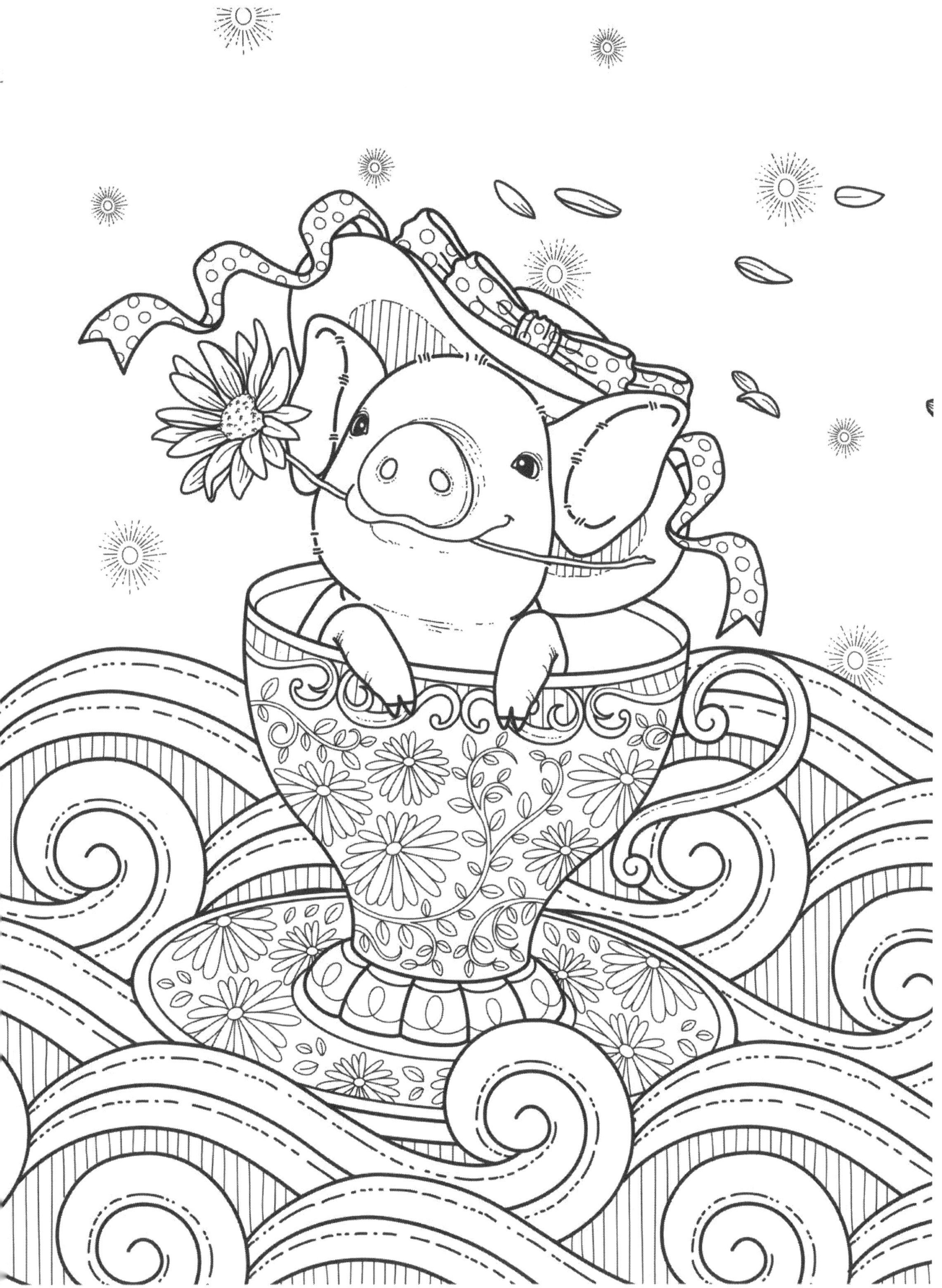

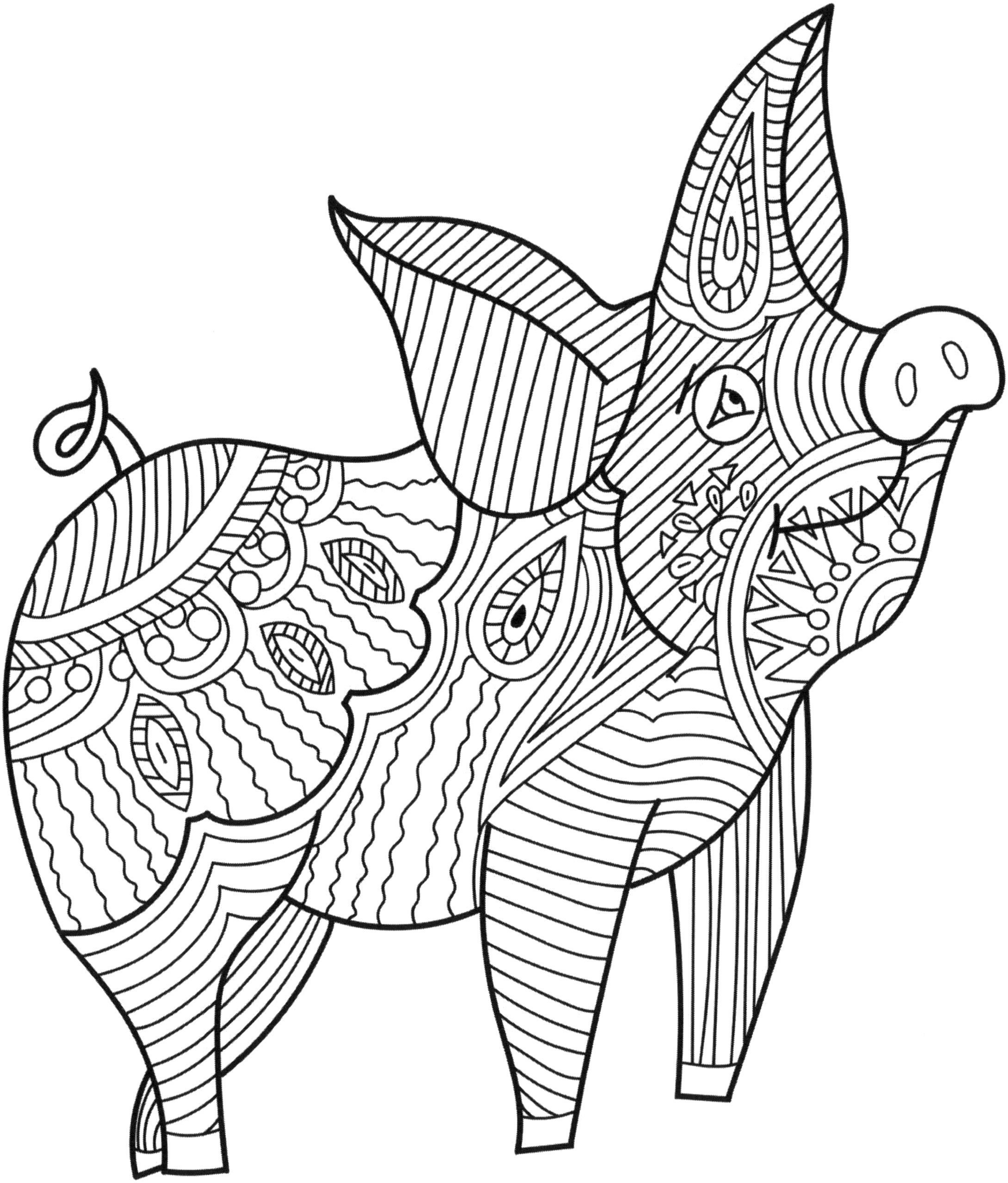

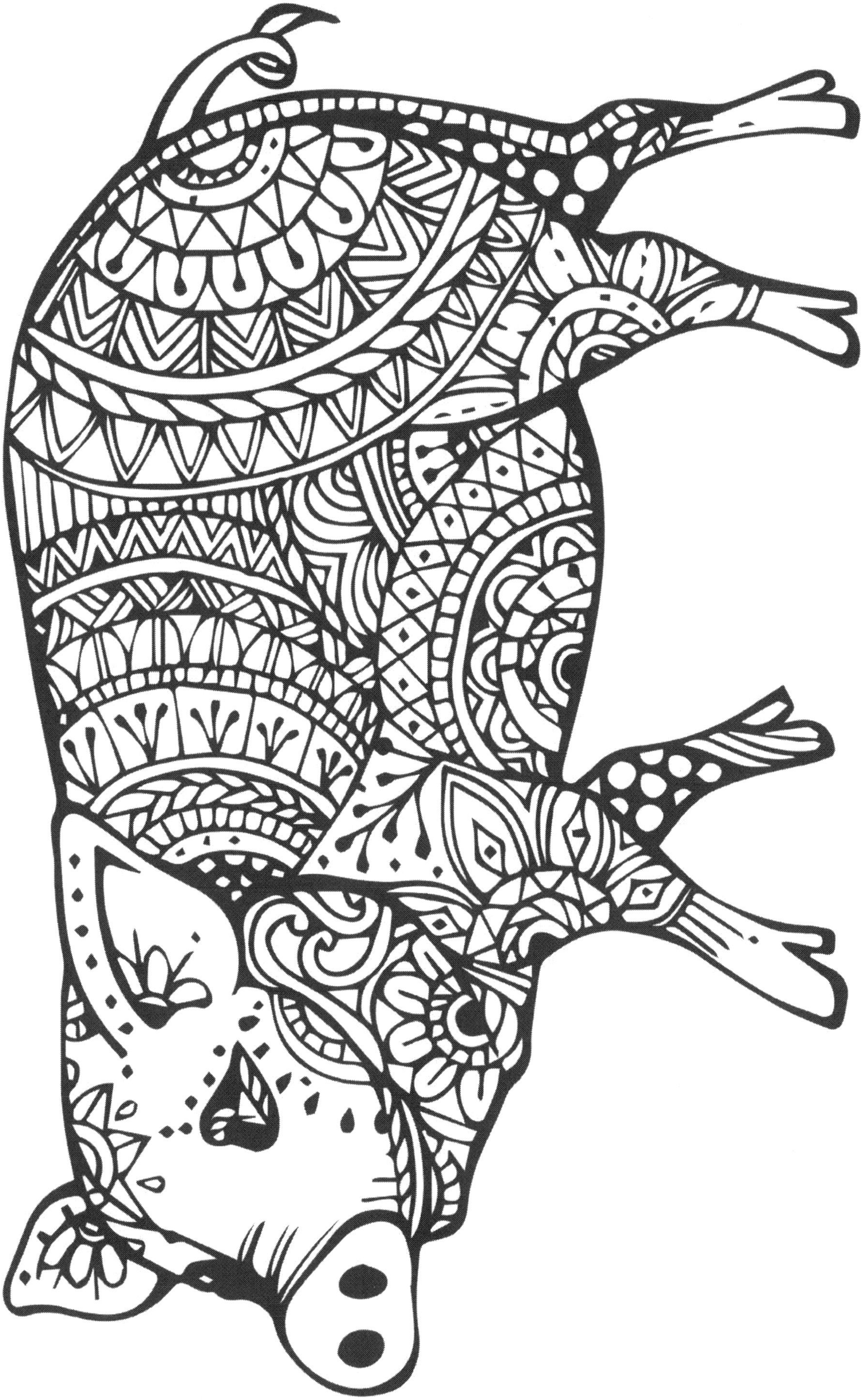

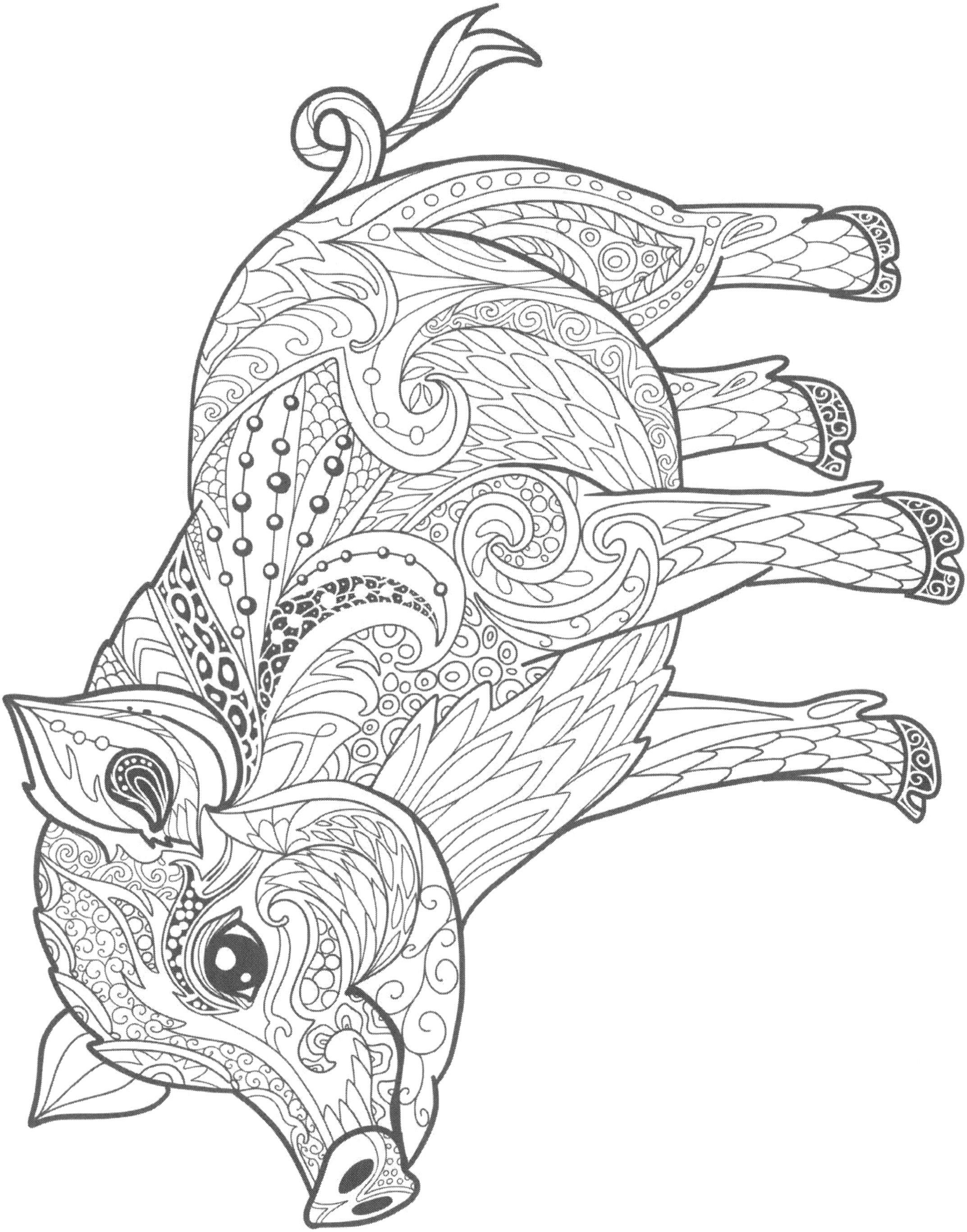

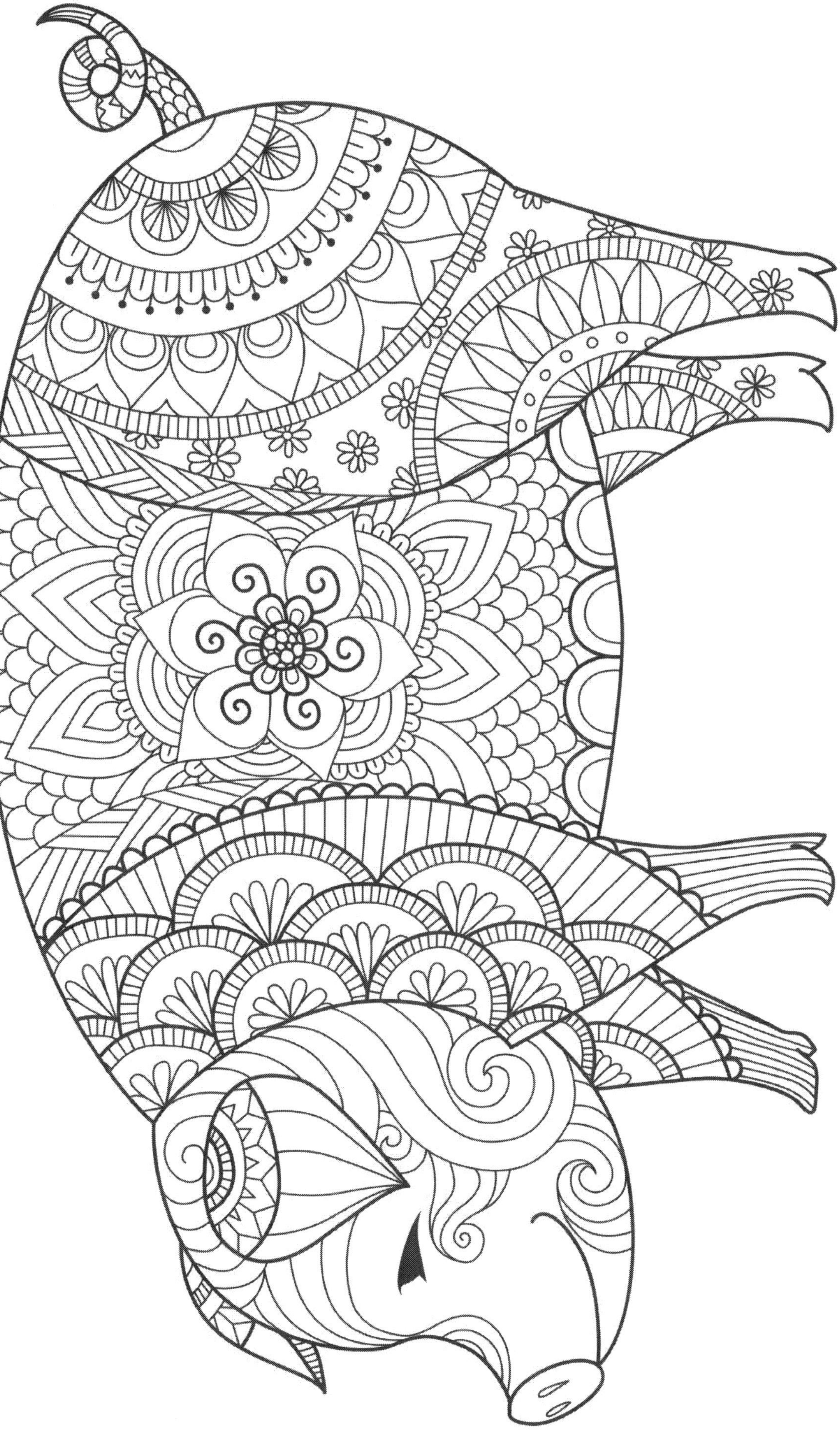

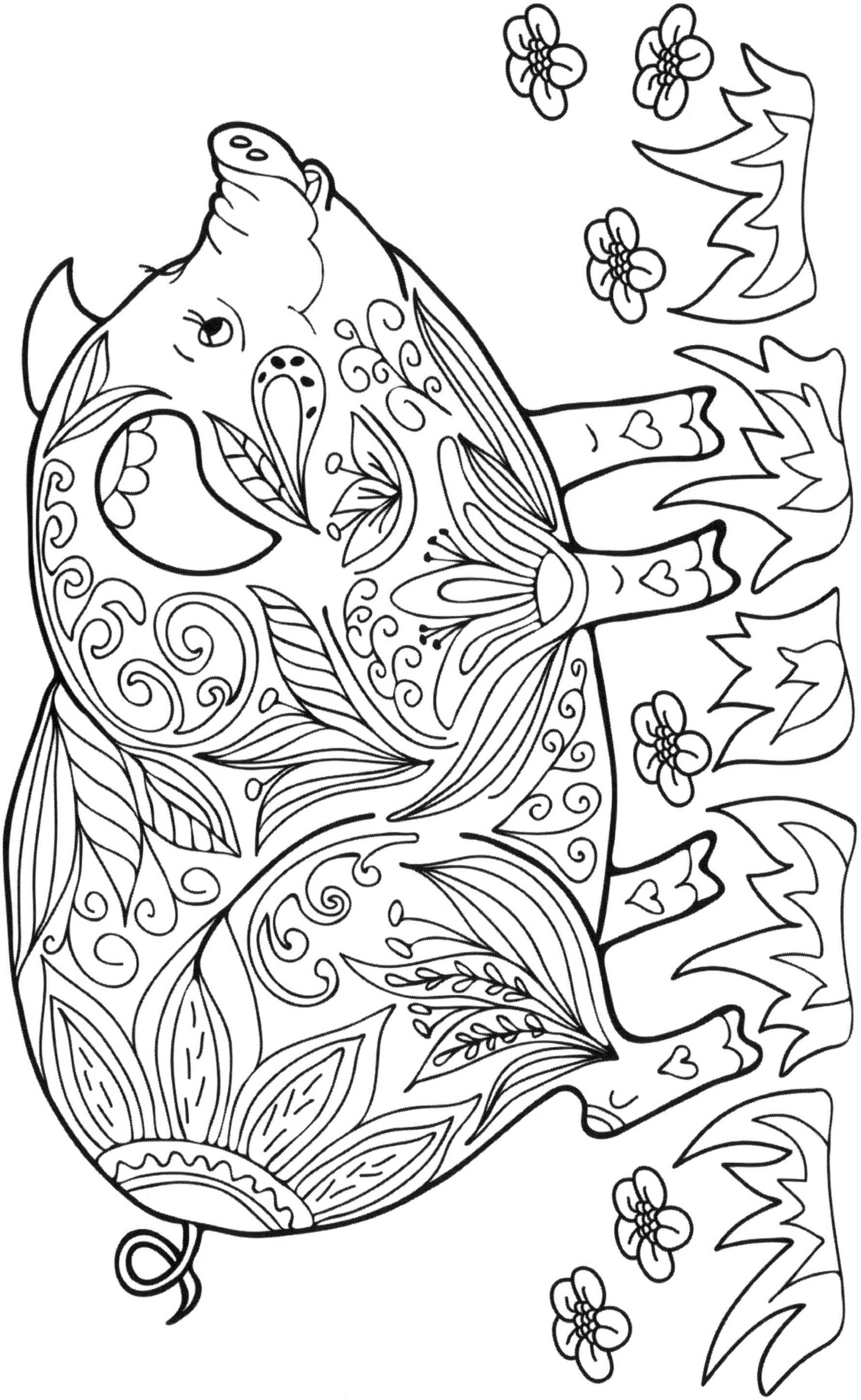

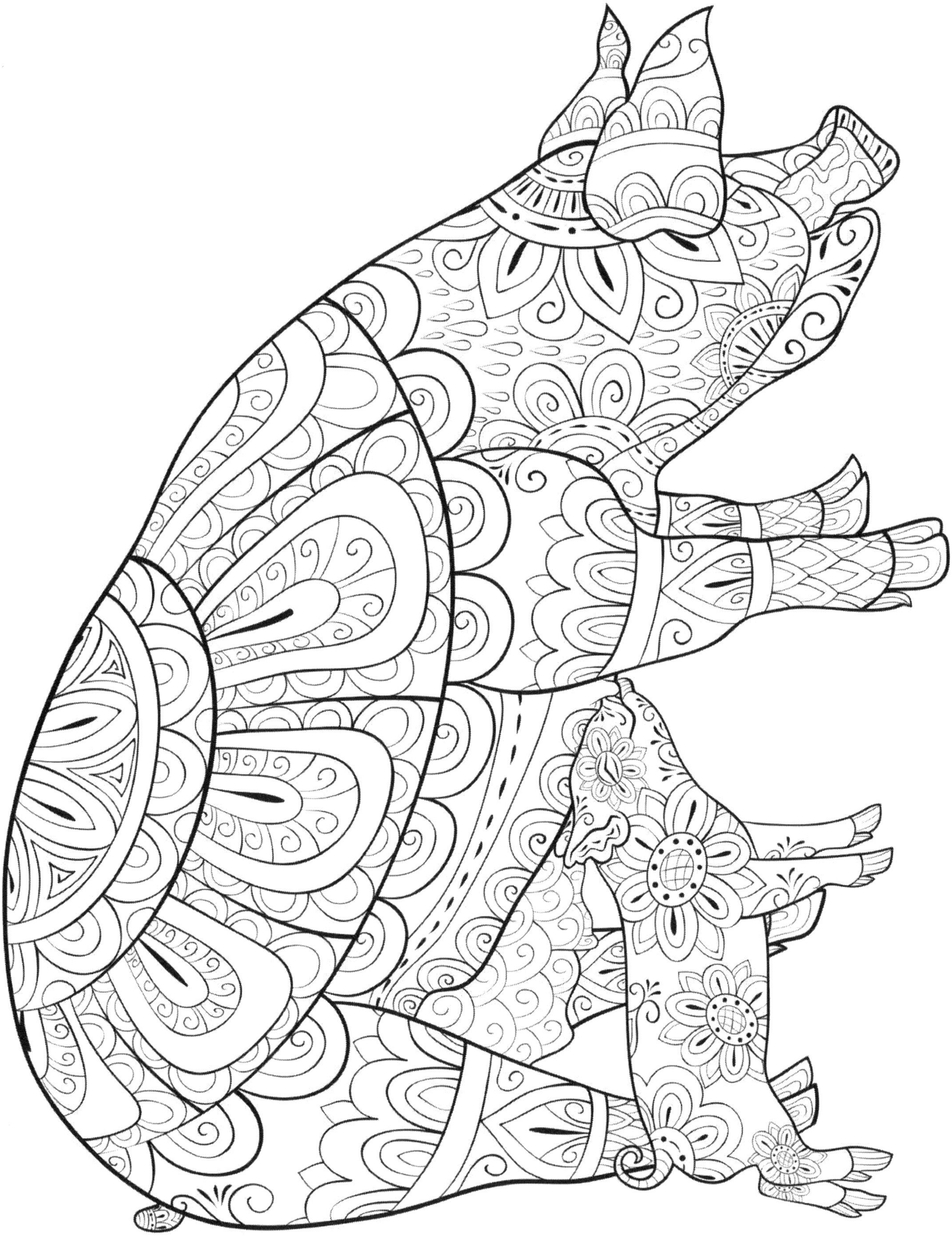

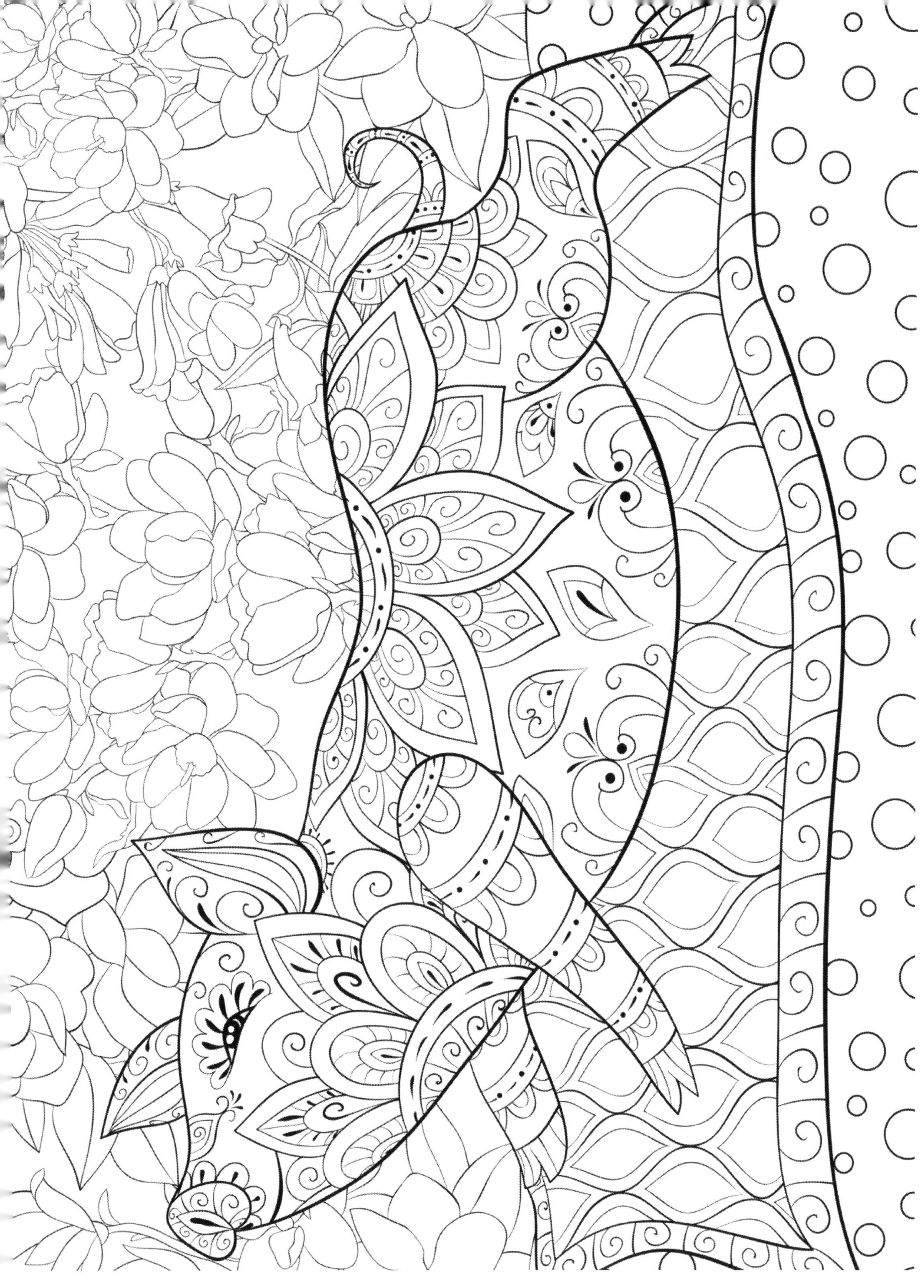

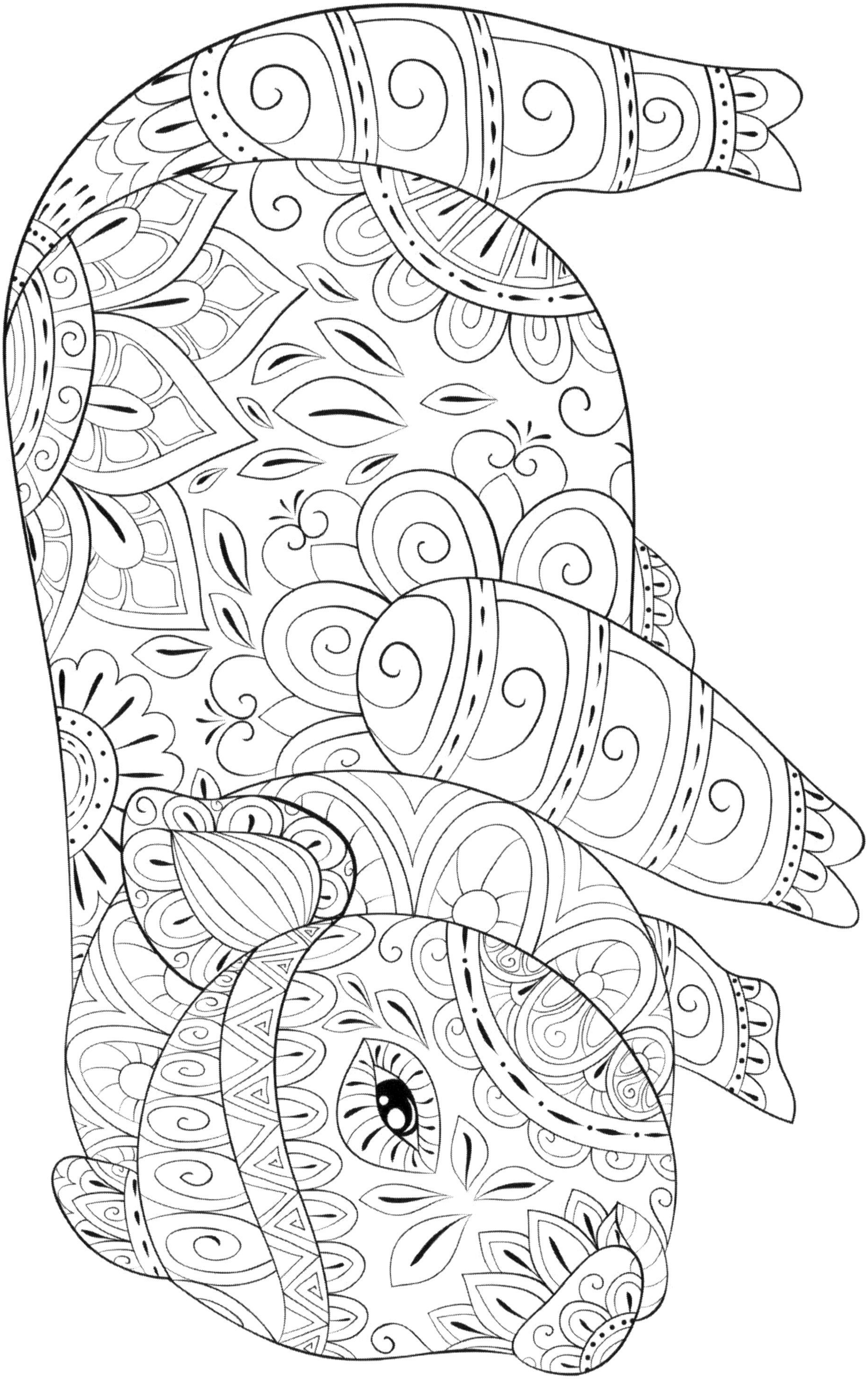

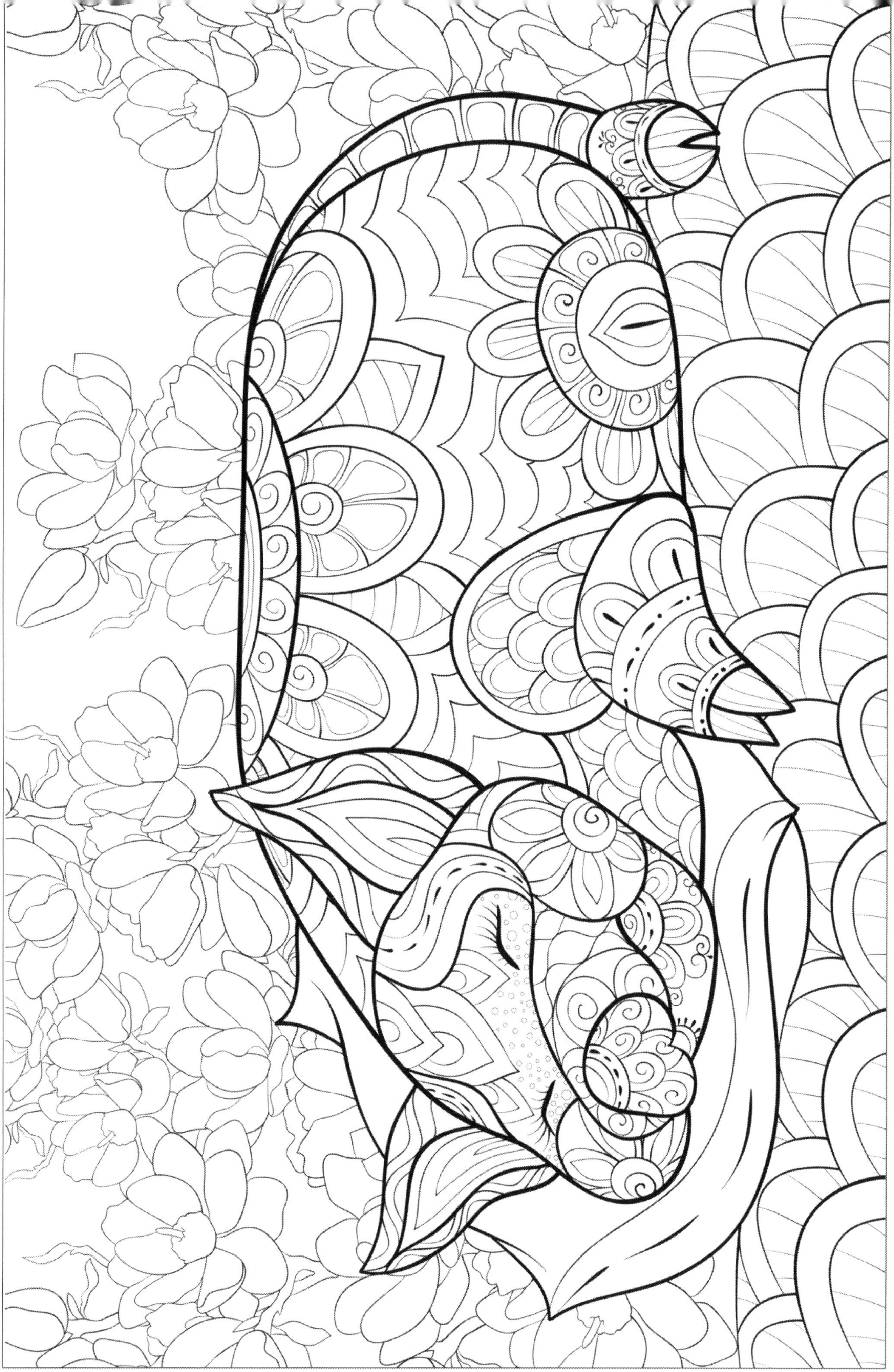

Made in the USA
Columbia, SC
11 July 2024

38498374R00030